Are You In Control Finances?
If not, would you like to be?

Personal finances have been a challenge for too many people for too long. Few people were trained in the money game growing up. In this, easy to read and informative Itty Bitty® book, Akemi Clauson maps out the best way to understand money and obtain financial freedom. The 15 steps in this book will guide you in creating a simple system to take control of your money.

In this book you will learn:

- How to Eliminate Debt
- How to Create a Simple Budget
- How to Protect Your Assets and Loved Ones
- And so much more!

If it's time for you to take charge of your money and have a financially free future, pick up a copy of this Itty Bitty® book today!

Your Amazing Itty Bitty® Financial Fitness Book

15 Steps to Financial Freedom

Akemi Clauson

Published by Itty Bitty® Publishing
A subsidiary of S & P Productions, Inc.

Printed in the United States of America

Itty Bitty Publishing
311 Main Street, Suite D
El Segundo, CA 90245
(310) 640-8885

ISBN: 978-1-950326-15-0

Dedication

This book is dedicated to my kind and patient husband, Paul, who has always encouraged me to pursue my passion of helping people by teaching the basics of personal finance. He is my number one fan, always cheering me on. I love the life he and I have built together.

This book is also dedicated to my amazing grandson, Kody. At an early age he became interested in investing. One day, he handed me an envelope filled with cash and said, "Grandma, I want to invest in mutual funds." That was music to my ears! He was only eleven years old! He had saved most of the money he had received for birthdays and holidays, as well as his allowance money. I am so proud of him!

In addition, I would like to dedicate this book to all the fabulous and incredible flight attendants at United Airlines. I hope to see you again in the future in the friendly skies.

Finally, I would also like to thank my dear friend, Karen Garland for all her help. She didn't hesitate to say, "Yes!" when I asked her if she would be willing to help me. She took the time to read my drafts and gave me her feedback. I cherish the friendship we've shared for the past twenty-five years.

Stop by our Itty Bitty® website to find interesting blog entries regarding financial information at:

www.IttyBittyPublishing.com

Or visit Akemi Clauson at

www.icarefinancial.net

Table of Contents

Introduction

What does financial freedom look like to you? Is it being debt-free? Is it not having to live paycheck to paycheck? Financial freedom looks different for everyone. For me, it is all about having financial peace of mind, not having to worry or stress about money, and having enough money saved for a comfortable retirement when the time comes.

According to surveys:

- Eight out of 10 American workers (78%) are living paycheck to paycheck (CareerBuilder, 2017).
- One in three Americans between ages 55 and 64 have no retirement savings. Those who do have savings, have a median value of $120,000 (Federal Reserve Board, 2015).
- Nearly half of American households (40%) said they wouldn't be able to cover a $400 emergency without borrowing money or selling something (Federal Reserve Board, 2014).
- More than half of Americans (65%) are losing sleep over money worries (Credit Cards.com, 2017).

It's sad but true . . . and I can relate. I was a single mom (divorced with two kids), and I lived paycheck to paycheck most of my adult life. I was constantly broke and in debt. I would max out my credit cards, close the accounts and eventually pay them off, only to again max out new cards. It was a vicious cycle. I felt stressed and overwhelmed. Finally, I made the decision to become debt-free once and for all. One December night, I sat at my dining table and made a list of all my debts and their balances. It came to a little over $22,000. I came up with a plan and the following month, January, I began paying off my debts aggressively.

While I was paying off my debts, I studied and educated myself about personal finance. I read every personal finance book I could get my hands on. I read about budgeting, credit, investing, mutual funds, mortgages, 401(k) plans, IRA's, etc. The more I read, the more passionate I became about personal finance.

Twenty-one months later I became debt-free! It was exciting! It was exhilarating! It was as if a ton of bricks had fallen off my shoulders. I felt FREE! It was truly an empowering experience.

Six months before I became debt-free, I married my husband. We've continued to live a debt-free life together, including our mortgage.

The content of this book is meant to be strictly educational in nature, and my own personal opinion. I am not rendering any legal, financial, or tax advice. Please seek the advice of an attorney, a CPA, or a fee-only financial advisor if such service is needed.

Step 1
Know Your Worth

Before embarking on your journey to financial freedom, you need to know where you are now, financially speaking, in order to get to your destination. The best way to know your current financial situation is to calculate your net worth by doing the following:

1. On a blank piece of paper, draw a vertical line in the middle to make two columns.
2. At the top of the paper write "Net Worth as of (current date)".
3. In the left column, list everything you OWN (assets), and the dollar value next to each item.
4. In the right column, list everything you OWE (liabilities) and the amount next to each item.
5. Add each column and write the total amount at the bottom of each column.
6. Subtract your total liabilities from your total assets.
7. The answer is your net worth. (Assets minus Liabilities = Net Worth)
8. Repeat this process every year.

Net Worth Does Not Equal Self-Worth

- Net worth is simply a snapshot of your finances in a moment of time.
- Net worth is fluid. It changes from year to year, month to month, week to week, or even day to day.
- Net worth gives you a reference point for measuring your progress toward achieving your financial goals.
- A negative net worth indicates you are insolvent, meaning you are unable to repay all your debts.
- A positive number indicates you're solvent; you have enough resources to meet all your debt obligations.

Examples of assets (things you own):

- money in your checking account
- money in your savings account
- value of your retirement accounts
- value of your brokerage accounts
- your house, rental homes
- antiques, jewelry, collectibles

Examples of liabilities (what you owe):

- mortgage loan
- car loan
- student loan
- credit card, retail card balances
- personal loan
- all consumer loans

Step 2
Save For A Rainy Day

When you are not prepared for unexpected emergencies that life throws at you every now and then, you get into trouble. Unforeseen things happen, and sometimes, when it rains it pours! In order to succeed financially, you need to be prepared for major unexpected expenses that pop up every now and then by doing the following:

1. Save *at least* three to six months' worth of your monthly expenses.
2. If saving three to six months' worth of expenses is not possible right now, save one thousand dollars. This amount will still be helpful if you should need, for example, new tires, or have your water heater repaired.
3. When you withdraw money from your emergency fund, be sure to replenish the withdrawn amount over a period of time (the sooner the better).
4. Never touch this money unless it's a true emergency!

You Are Not Alone

If you have no rainy-day fund, you are not alone. According to the recent Federal Reserve Economic Survey, almost half of American households said they cannot cover an emergency expense of $400 without borrowing money or selling something.

Here are some ways you can kick-start your emergency fund:

- Go through your whole house and gather anything you no longer need or want and sell it at a garage sale, on Craig's List, or similar sites. Deposit the money you made from the sale of the items into an emergency fund.
- Take one or two dollars every single day and put it into a jar or an envelope. At the end of the month take it to the bank and deposit it into your emergency fund.
- Save all coins you get back in change. Every few months or so deposit the coins into your emergency fund.
- Deposit your tax refunds into the emergency fund.
- Get a temporary, part-time job or a side hustle and deposit all the income from it into your emergency fund.

Step 3
Save for Your Future

One of the best ways to save for your future is with a 401(k)-like plan. This is a great plan because the money is deducted automatically from your paycheck, making it effortless for you to save. Another benefit is that the amount being deducted from your paycheck is not taxed and your money will grow tax-deferred until you withdraw the money at retirement.

1. Check to see if your employer offers 401(k), 403(b), 457, or a Thrift Savings Plan (TSP).
2. If your employer offers one of the above plans, ask if there is an employer match.
3. Strive to contribute at least 10 to 20% of your gross income. Contribute the maximum amount if possible.
4. If you cannot contribute 10 to 20%, then contribute at least up to the employer match. That's free money!
5. Every six months or every year, increase the contribution amount by one percent until you reach 20% or higher.
6. Never cash out your 401(k) money when changing jobs. Roll it over into your new employer's 401(k) plan or into an IRA.
7. Do not borrow from your 401(k).

What to Do if Your Workplace Doesn't Offer an Employer-Sponsored Retirement Plan

- Open a Roth IRA or traditional IRA.
- Roth IRA contributions are made with post (after) tax money so there is no tax benefit when you contribute; however, the money grows and comes out tax-free.
- Contributions to a traditional IRA are made with pre (before) tax money which means the contributions are not taxed; however, the withdrawals at age 59 ½ or later will be taxed.
- Open your IRA at a discount brokerage firm (for example: Fidelity, Schwab, Vanguard).
- Don't invest in individual stocks (too risky).
- Invest in mutual funds for diversification (don't put all your eggs in one basket).
- Invest in index funds to keep fees low.
- Keep it simple by investing in a target-date fund, also called a lifecycle fund.
- Use dollar-cost averaging, which is an investment strategy where you invest a fixed amount of money at regular intervals such as weekly, monthly, or quarterly to reduce the impact of market volatility.

Step 4
Eliminate Debts

Debt is a deterrent to your financial health. Strive to pay it off as soon as possible, especially consumer debt. The best way to pay off your debts is by the debt snowball method. The idea is to focus on one debt at a time.

1. Make a list of all your debts and balances in the order of smallest to largest.
2. Pay the minimum amount due on each debt except for the smallest debt.
3. Add as much extra money as you can to expedite the debt payoff even more.
4. Pay the minimum amount due PLUS the extra amount on the first smallest debt.
5. When the first smallest debt is paid off, take the amount you were paying toward the first debt and add it to the minimum amount due on the next smallest debt.
6. Continue in this way until all your debts are paid off.
7. Stop charging while paying off debts.

I had a little over $22,000 of debt when I made the decision to become debt-free once and for all. Using the snowball method, I paid off my debts in 21 months.

"The Borrower Is a Slave to the Lender and the Debtor to the Creditor."
Benjamin Franklin

Some financial experts believe it's better to pay the debt with the highest interest rate first, known as the avalanche method. It's true you would save more money on interest using this method. However:

- You quickly get a small victory by paying off your first (smallest) debt faster by using the snowball method.
- Paying off debt is hard, and it takes time. You achieve a small victory every time you pay off one debt.
- You gain momentum with each paid-off debt. One down, three to go! Two down, two to go! Three down, one to go! It's empowering! That's how it was for me when I was paying off my debts.
- You can choose either method you prefer. The important thing is to simply start and stay the course. Don't give up!

Step 5
Create a Simple Budget

A budget is simply a spending plan, and it's essential for your financial success. Budgeting helps you achieve your financial goals.

1. List all your monthly *net* income.
2. List all your monthly *fixed* expenses. For bills you receive once a year, divide the amount by 12 to get a monthly average.
3. List all *variable* and *discretionary* expenses.
4. Group similar expenses and categorize them, such as food, entertainment, utilities, supplies, gifts, health, etc. Allocate a dollar amount to each category.
5. Subtract your total monthly expenses from your total monthly net income.
6. If you have money left over, it can go toward your savings, debt repayment, or you can spend it as you please. If you get a negative number, you need to cut back on some of your discretionary expenses.

Today there are many budgeting apps such as Mint, Quicken, YNAB (You Need a Budget), or Personal Capital that make budgeting easy.

Different Ways to Budget

50/30/20 Plan:

- 50% goes to NEEDS (rent, utilities, bills, etc.)
- 30% on FUN (eat out, Netflix, spa, designer shoes, vacations, etc.)
- 20% goes to DEBT and SAVINGS. If you have no debt, all 20% goes to savings. If you do have debt, 20% goes to debt, or you can split between the two.

Expense Tracking Method:
I no longer allocate certain amounts of money to each category. I simply track all my monthly income and expenses. Just by tracking, I see where my money is going and how much I'm spending each month. I only care that my expenses are less than income. I find this way of budgeting to be more flexible and easier to manage. I use Quicken, which makes expense tracking simple and hassle-free.

Envelope System:
Allocate sums of money for discretionary or variable expenses (food, movies, etc.), put the cash in envelopes and label them. Spend only the money you have in the envelopes. Monitor amounts in each envelope during the month. When the envelope becomes empty, that's it. No more spending for that category. However, you may borrow from another envelope if money is still available.

Step 6
Take Care of Your Credit

Credit impacts your life in many ways. If you have poor credit, it will be harder for you to:

1. Qualify for a mortgage
2. Rent a place to live
3. Get a car loan
4. Get a credit card
5. Get a cellphone plan
6. Rent a car

Some car rental companies will accept debit cards but it's a bit of a hassle, as you'll have to jump through the hoops. Some will put a hold on funds in your account (you can't use the funds) and you will need to provide extra documents.

As you can see, credit affects your life in major ways! It's important to establish and maintain good credit. You'll pay less for everything with good credit because of the lower interest rate you'll be offered on various loans and credit cards. Also, in most states, insurance companies charge higher premiums to customers with poor credit than to those with good credit.
When used responsibly, credit is an excellent financial tool.

Factors That Affect Your Credit Score

There are many credit scores, but the crème de la crème of credit scores is the FICO score. It is a score used by most lenders. The five major factors that affect your FICO scores are:

- Payment history: A whopping 35% of your score comes from timely payments. Always pay your bills on time!
- Amount of debt: This is another big factor as 30% of your score comes from debt utilization (debt ratio) which is the amount of debt relative to your available credit. Keep your utilization below 30%.
- Length of history: The older the credit the better, as 15% of your score comes from how long you've had your credit. Therefore, don't close your old credit card even if you are no longer using it.
- Types of credit. Only 10% of your score comes from this. It's good to have a variety of credit such as a car loan, mortgage, and credit cards but if you only have one type of credit, I wouldn't worry about it.
- New credit. The final 10% of your score comes from new credit. Avoid applying for too much credit in a short period of time. For instance, if you applied for a credit card in January, wait until July or August to finance a car or apply for another credit card.

Step 7
Save For Big Purchases

Are you dreaming of a white sandy beach, turquoise blue water, and sipping Mai Tais? It's fun to dream of a relaxing, tropical vacation. Well, you CAN go on your tropical vacation as long as you plan for it in advance. Whether you want to go on vacation or buy a home appliance or a car, the key is to start saving for it. Here's how:

1. Decide what you want to buy.
2. Research how much it will cost.
3. Decide how much you want to spend.
4. Decide when you want to buy it.
5. Divide the cost by how many months you have until your purchase date. For example: you want to buy a new sofa set. You research the cost online and also check out local furniture stores. You decide to spend about $1,200. You want to buy it in a year. You divide $1,200 by 12 (months) which equals 100. You need to save $100 per month for one year. If you want to buy it in six months, you'll need to save $200 per month for six months ($1200 divided by 6 = 200).

You Can Have Anything You Want, Just Not All at the Same Time

You want many things. I know. You want to go on a vacation, but you also want the latest new iPhone. Which do you want more? It's all about prioritizing your goals.

- On a piece of paper, list everything you want to do or buy.
- Arrange them in the order of importance or urgency. For example: you want to buy a new laptop, but your refrigerator is on its last leg. The refrigerator is more urgent than your laptop.
- Put a price tag next to each item.
- Write the desired purchase date for each item.
- Pick the first item to purchase and divide the cost by the number of months to know how much to save each month.
- Go down the list and do the same for everything on your list.

Many years ago, my husband and I talked about going to Maui on a vacation. We decided to save $200 every month for one year. At the end of the year, we had $2,400. We used our credit card to pay for everything while we were in Maui, and we paid it off when we got home. Let me tell you, having the money saved in advance made it the best vacation ever!

Step 8
Distinguish Between Good and Bad Debt

I encourage you to pay off your debt because debt is a barrier to accumulating wealth. With that said, not all debts are bad. There are good debts and bad debts. It's important to know the difference.

Good debts <u>appreciate</u>, or go up in value over time, such as:

1. Mortgage
2. Home equity loan used for home improvement or remodeling
3. Education
4. Business

Bad debts <u>depreciate</u>, or go down in value over time, such as:

1. Credit card debt
2. Consumer debt
3. Car loan
4. Cash advance

Debt Costs Money

Debt is not free. It comes with a cost by way of finance charges you must pay. However, there are advantages to good debts mentioned earlier.

Advantages of good debt:

- Mortgage: gives you the ability to purchase your home and start building equity.
- Home equity loan: home improvement or remodeling increases the home value.
- Education: a person with a bachelor's degree earns over $24,000 MORE per year than a person with only a high school degree (2017 College Board research).
- Business: produces income, loan is tax deductible and profits are all yours to keep unlike receiving salary or wages.

Car loan is technically a bad debt, but it is a necessity in order for you to drive to work. Keep your payments low by purchasing a reliable, modest car.

A word of caution: A good debt can become a bad debt if you overextend yourself. Borrow *only* what you need. Do not buy too big of a house, or too fancy of a car just because you were approved for a bigger loan amount.

Step 9
Pay off Credit Cards in Full Each Month

Yes, credit cards are convenient, but they are expensive. You learned in Step 8 that credit card debt is bad debt. You should strive to pay off your credit card balances in full every single month for the following reasons:

1. Credit card debt is one of the most expensive debts to carry with an average interest rate of around 17 percent.
2. Having too much debt relative to your available credit hurts your credit score. For instance, let's say you have a credit card with an available credit of $5,000, and your outstanding balance is $2,000. That is a 40% utilization (debt ratio), which will lower your credit score. Keep your debt ratio below 30%.
3. The notion that carrying a balance helps your credit score is a myth. You do NOT need to carry a balance in order to have a good credit score.
4. Paying off a credit card in full saves you money as you'll pay no finance charges.

Pros and Cons of Using a Credit Card

According to the 2019 Experian Consumer Credit Review, average Americans have four credit cards. There are both pros and cons to using credit cards.

Pros:
- Convenience. There's no need to carry a lot of cash. Most merchants today accept credit card payments.
- Expense tracking. You can easily track your expenses through your statements.
- Purchase protection. If you want to dispute a charge or return a defective product and get a refund, your credit card issuer will help you. If you paid by cash, check, or debit card you're on your own.
- Builds good credit history. Paying for your purchases by credit card and making timely payments will raise your credit score.

Cons:
- Easy to overspend. There is too much temptation to overspend, as you don't feel the pain when paying with credit cards.
- Finance charge. When you carry a balance, you pay a finance charge.
- Fees. There are various fees such as late fee, over-the-limit fee, balance transfer fee, etc., making your purchases more expensive.

Step 10
Be on the Same Page with Your Spouse

Arguing over money is the number one reason married couples divorce in America. Couples need to be in sync regarding money in order to have a happy and healthy relationship. Communication is the key.

1. Set up a time and place to discuss your finances. If you have small children, send them to their grandparents or plan the talk after they have gone to bed.
2. Plan the talk when there are no financial issues at the moment, such as overdrawn accounts or late payments of bills.
3. Talk openly and honestly about your dreams and goals.
4. Do not be judgmental. This is the time to really *listen* to each other.
5. Be honest about any concerns you have. If you're often late in paying your bills discuss what you can do together to change that.
6. Come up with a budget or a spending plan that works for both of you.
7. Plan together for big purchases such as a home appliance, car, vacation, etc.

Financial Infidelity Can Ruin a Marriage

According to a 2020 survey by Creditcard.com, 44% of people surveyed admitted to hiding a credit card or bank account from their partners. Spouses and partners commit financial infidelity in the following ways:

- Hiding receipts for purchases
- Lying about the purchase price
- Saying the item was on sale when it was not
- Pretending the newly purchased item is an old purchase
- Taking money from savings account without telling your spouse
- Opening a credit card account without telling your spouse
- Hiding credit card statements

If you/your spouse have done any of the above, it's time to fess up. It's time to have a serious talk about honestly managing the family finances.

- Make a promise to each other to be transparent about money.
- Give each other a monthly allowance where each can spend freely with no questions asked.
- Every month go over your expenses; look over the bank and credit card statements together.

Step 11
Beware of Cosigning

Cosigning for a loan is fraught with peril. When you cosign, you are agreeing to be responsible for the repayment of the loan should the borrower default on the loan. There are many risks involved with co-signing:

1. Your credit score will take a hit if the borrower is late or misses a payment.
2. Your credit score will take a hit if the loan raises your credit utilization ratio, meaning you've borrowed too much relative to your available credit.
3. You may be denied a loan due to high debt-to-income ratio and/or high credit utilization rate.
4. You are responsible for paying back the loan if the signer (borrower) of the loan stops making payments.
5. You can't remove yourself as a co-signer; once you've agreed to co-sign, you're tied to the loan until it is paid off.
6. The relationship may be ruined if the borrower defaults on the loan.

When Is It Okay to Cosign?

You may wish to help a friend or a family member by cosigning *if*:

- You are willing and *able* to make the payments should the borrower default on the loan.
- The payments will not impact your lifestyle.
- The payments will not keep you from contributing to your retirement plans.
- The payments will not put your retirement security at risk.
- If the borrower defaults, you are willing to consider the unpaid balance to be a gift to the borrower and not become resentful.

If you decide to cosign, I suggest the following:

- Open an online account to view the statements regularly.
- Have the lender notify you immediately when the payment is not made by the due date.
- Communicate with the signer (borrower) regularly.

OR:

- Make the payments yourself to avoid hurting your credit, and have the borrower pay you directly.

Step 12
Spend Less Than You Earn

"Spend less than you earn," is such a simple concept and yet so hard to do. Here are a few tips for getting started:

1. Pay yourself first (before the money slips away from you).
2. Have an emergency fund.
3. Track your expenses carefully.
4. Do less eating out and takeout.
5. Make a list before going to a grocery store; buy only the items on the list.
6. Brown bag your lunch to work.
7. If you see an item you want to buy, wait a few days to see if you still want it.

Are your expenses still higher than your income? Here are some ideas to bring in extra money:

1. Ask for overtime at work, if possible.
2. Get a side hustle (Uber or Lyft driver, pizza delivery, etc.).
3. Baby sit, house sit, pet sit.
4. Tutor or give lessons (guitar, piano, etc.).
5. Change your mindset: less is more.

The Power of Delayed Gratification

We live in a consumer-oriented society. We are bombarded with commercials and advertisements all day long. You need to practice self-control for your financial well-being. *The ability to delay gratification is essential to your success.*

- Stanford University did an experiment on delayed gratification in 1972.
- A researcher placed one marshmallow in front of four- and five-year old children and told them that if they would wait until later to eat it, they'd get another marshmallow. (The researcher left the room and told the kids he would be back in 15 minutes).
- The minute the researcher left the room and closed the door, some children ate the marshmallow right away.
- Other children waited and waited but ultimately couldn't wait any longer and ate the marshmallow before the researcher returned.
- Still other children waited patiently until the researcher returned to the room and they were given a second marshmallow.

The researchers did a follow-up on these children for 40 years. They found that the children who patiently waited to get two marshmallows were more successful in their careers, relationships and life in general compared to those who did not. Lesson learned: patience is key to your success.

Step 13
Protect Your Assets and Loved Ones

You've worked hard to build a secure future. Now you need to protect your assets and your family. There are five types of insurance you need to have:

1. **Life insurance**. If you have anyone who is dependent on your income, such as your spouse or minor children, you need life insurance (level term life insurance).
2. **Health insurance**. You need health insurance to cover medical costs for you and your family. The number one cause of bankruptcies in the United States is healthcare costs.
3. **Auto insurance**. It is illegal to drive without auto insurance in most states.
4. **Homeowner's insurance**. If you own a home, you need to have homeowner's insurance, even if it's paid off. Your home is most likely your largest asset. You need to guard against financial risk.
5. **Disability insurance**. Your ability to earn money is your greatest asset. You have a higher chance of being injured than of dying. Protect your income.

Estate Planning Is Essential

Estate planning is about preparing for unavoidable occurrences such as death or incapacitation. Estate planning involves having a collection of legal documents such as:

- Will or trust documents
- Durable financial power of attorney
- Durable healthcare power of attorney
- Advance health directive

What do these documents do?

- A <u>will</u> lets your family know how you want your assets to be distributed. It's about who gets what after you die. A will must go through probate which costs money and time. A <u>trust</u> avoids probate. You control the trust while you are alive.
- The <u>durable financial power of attorney</u> gives the appointed person the authority to manage your finances while you are incapacitated and can no longer manage on your own.
- <u>Durable healthcare power of attorney</u> gives the appointed person the authority to speak for you about your treatments when you are unable to do so. An <u>advance health directive</u> lets your family know your wishes for end-of-life decisions.

Step 14
Automate Your Finances

Automating your finances makes managing your money and your life much simpler.

1. Request for direct deposit of your paychecks if your company offers it. Arrange to have a portion of your pay go directly into your emergency savings account (out of sight, out of mind).
2. Set up an automatic monthly transfer from your checking account into your investment accounts, such as a Roth IRA or traditional IRA.
3. Set up an automatic monthly transfer from your checking account into your sinking fund account. This account could be for future purchases, such as a car, vacation, home appliance, etc.
4. Set up an autopay for all your recurring bills, such as your mortgage payments, utilities, insurance premiums, car loan, cellphones, internet, etc., from your checking account or credit card.
5. Monitor your bank balances regularly.

Advantages of Automating Your Finances

- You will never miss a payment or be late, which will help you avoid costly penalties and late fees.
- Savings will be consistent and easy. You won't be tempted to spend the money first and then try to save whatever is left over, if anything.
- You will be practicing dollar-cost averaging which is a great way to invest. You will buy more shares when prices are down and buy less shares when prices are up.
- You can enjoy spending the surplus money guilt-free knowing that you've taken care of all your bills, savings, and investments.
- Your credit score will improve due to timely payments of your recurring bills with autopay.
- You will avoid stress, and gain peace of mind when your finances are automated.
- It frees up your time for other enjoyable activities.

As you can see, there are many advantages to automating your finances. You must be diligent, however, about monitoring your bank account balances regularly to ensure that you have enough funds to cover all your bills, savings, and investments.

Step 15
Believe in Yourself! You've Got This!

In order to succeed in anything in life, you must first believe in yourself. Here are a few ideas if you are facing thoughts of self-doubt:

1. Surround yourself with positive people.
2. Be inspired by reading books and blogs, listening to podcasts, or watching documentaries about people who have overcome adversity.
3. Choose friends who will encourage you and build you up.
4. Pay attention to your inner thoughts such as "I'll fail," or "I can't do it." Replace them with positive words such as, "If I fail, I'll just keep trying," or, "I'll never know until I try."
5. As Nike ads say: "Just do it!" What have you got to lose? (Maybe debts?)
6. Remember the words of British poet Alfred Lord Tennyson, "It's better to have tried and failed than to live life wondering what would've happened if I had tried."

"I Am the Master of My Fate: Captain of My Soul." *~ William Ernest Henley*

According to Julian B. Rotter, American psychologist, individuals with *internal locus of control*:

- Believe consequences and outcomes are results of their own actions.
- Take responsibility for life's negative events and circumstances in their lives rather than blame outside forces.
- Believe they have control over their circumstances and have a choice in their lives.
- Foster self-efficacy (power to effect change).

Research has shown that people with *internal locus of control* tend to be happier and less stressed, unlike those with *external locus of control* who believe their circumstances are due to outside forces (victim mentality).

Strive to:

- Understand there are things in life you can and cannot control.
- Focus on things you *can* control.
- Understand life has peaks and valleys.
- Learn from your mistakes.
- Take responsibility for your actions.

You've finished. Before you go...

Tweet/share that you finished this book.

Please star rate this book.

Reviews are solid gold to writers. Please take a few minutes to give us some itty bitty feedback.

ABOUT THE AUTHOR

It was after a difficult marriage ended at age 26, that I found myself in financial straits needing to support myself and my two small children. I had to start from scratch as a waitress and eventually found myself $22,000 in debt. Through a lot of soul searching and hard work I was able to pay off all my debts in twenty-one months. By this time, I was working as a flight attendant for a major U.S. airline carrier.

When my coworkers learned of my success story, they began to confide in me their own financial hardships. I love sharing with them my personal finance knowledge gained over the years of paying off my debts. In fact, for the last couple of years I've been writing a monthly personal finance post for our flight attendant group on Facebook and have been gratified to hear that they are finding my posts helpful.

I am passionate about helping people, especially women and young people, by teaching them the basics of personal finance. I want to *inspire* those who have lost their spirit, *encourage* those who feel discouraged and *empower* those who feel powerless.

In 2017, I became a certified credit counselor. Two years later I was certified as a financial health counselor through National Association of Certified Credit Counselors (NACCC).

If you enjoyed this Itty Bitty Book you might also like...

- **Your Amazing Itty Bitty® Getting Financially Organized Trilogy** - Marie Burns

- **Your Amazing Itty Bitty® Book Of QuickBooks® Shortcuts** - By Barbara L. Starley

- **Your Amazing Itty Bitty® Business Experts Compilation Book** - Various Authors

Or any of the other Amazing Itty Bitty Books available online at www.ittybittypublishing.com.